Parents Coaching Parents

Other books
by Dennis E. Coates, Ph.D.

For parents:

Connect with Your Kid: Mastering the Top 10 Parent-Child Communication Skills

How Your Teen Can Grow a Smarter Brain: 7 Game-Changers That Will Maximize Your Teen's Brainpower—Permanently (second edition)

Preparing Your Teen for Life: 50 Insights to Help Your Child Grow Up Happy, Successful and Independent

Conversations with the Wise Uncle: The Secret to Being Strong as a Teenager and Preparing for Success as an Adult

Conversations with the Wise Aunt: The Secret to Being Strong as a Teenager and Preparing for Success as an Adult (with Kathleen Scott)

The Sacred Purpose: How Youth Sports Organizations Can Do More to Prepare Athletes for Life

For organizations:

Connect with Your Team: Mastering the Top 10 Communication Skills (with Meredith M. Bell)

Peer Coaching Made Simple

The Dark Secret of HRD: Four Things You Need to Know to Stop Wasting Money on Training

Poetry:

To the Colors (with Mark Hamilton)

Parents Coaching Parents

How Parents Can Help Each Other
Improve Family Communication Skills

Dennis E. Coates, Ph.D.

First Summit Publishing

1st / Summit \ Publishing

Parents Coaching Parents: How Parents Can Help Each Other Improve Family Communication Skills

Printed in the United States of America

First Summit Publishing
An imprint of Performance Support Systems, Inc.
757-873-3700

Cover and book design: Paula Schlauch

ISBN: 978-1-7348051-5-4

Quantity sales. Special discounts are available on quantity purchases by corporations, associations and others. For details, contact us at info@growstrongleaders.com or 757-656-4765.

For caring parents everywhere
...who are committed to
their kids' success

"Knowing is not enough;

we must apply.

Willing is not enough;

we must do."

—Bruce Lee

Contents

So You and Another Parent Decide to Coach Each Other

If you've never done this before, at first the idea of coaching someone might sound a little scary. Actually, all you'll be doing is giving support to another parent while the two of you work on skills to be more effective as you raise your kids to be happy, successful, independent adults. As you read this brief book, you're going to find out that you already know how to do most of what's needed. It's a lot like being a good friend. So there's no need to be nervous about it.

> As you read each chapter, notice how simple it is to coach another parent, and tell yourself: *I can do that.*

You don't need to be intimidated by the idea of being another parent's coach.

Yes, many people make coaching their profession: parent coaches, life coaches, athletic coaches, business coaches, executive coaches, trainers, counselors, consultants, therapists, and others. For sure, they've had plenty of education and training to prepare them for these careers.

Working with an experienced parent coach is an outstanding investment. But many parents can't afford to do this. For them, an effective, commonsense solution is to partner with another parent who is willing to be a coaching partner.

The idea that parents can coach each other is not revolutionary. Moms have been getting together to share their know-how with each other for...well, forever.

Today, this kind of helping activity is called "peer coaching." Coaching a parent who is working on being a better communicator is more like being a friend or a mentor. You do it because you care about their success. Very likely the parent who needs your help is someone you know well, such as your spouse, or another mom or dad.

The purpose of this book is to give you a few ideas to make your coaching interactions more effective.

To illustrate my suggestions, I've included sample coaching dialogues. The examples describe parents who are working on the skills that are explained in the book, *Connect with Your Kid: Mastering the Top 10 Parent-Child Communication Skills*. The book is a guide for improving what I've learned through the decades are the communication skills that matter most. A typical coaching process involves meeting regularly with the person you're coaching, reviewing what they committed to do in real-world situations, and talking about what they learned from these experiences. At the end of the meeting, you ask the person you're coaching to set new action goals to accomplish before the next meeting. And they do the same for you.

Your coaching is extremely helpful because reading a book like *Connect with Your Kid,* watching a video, or attending a parenting course is only the beginning. Once you learn what you should be doing, you need to make the skill your habitual response when interacting with your child. Realistically, replacing an old habit with a new skill takes time. It's like getting better at anything—it takes practice, practice, and more practice. It takes a lot of "reps" to stimulate your brain to rewire itself. Only then will you be comfortable responding automatically with an improved skill.

Along the way, this self-development effort can sometimes be frustrating. You might forget to apply the skill, or your initial attempts might feel awkward and ineffective. Even with good intentions and motivation, after a while you might get discouraged.

This is why it helps to have a coach.

To stay on track and master a skill, people benefit from having accountability, support, and encouragement. Very likely, this is why you and another person have decided to coach each other.

It's easier than you think to help someone become stronger as a parent.

It Really Is Simple... The 6 Basics of Parents Coaching Parents

To be a helpful coach to another parent, you don't need special training. All you need is the desire to be supportive and the willingness to put into practice some of the tips in this book. To boost your confidence, this brief guide will suggest ways to use skills you probably already have, such as holding someone accountable, listening, asking questions that get someone to think, and giving encouragement.

The person you're coaching may ask for your opinions, ideas, and help setting goals. As you interact with someone you're coaching, you may find it useful to refer to this book as you prepare to meet with them. Like the parent you're helping, the more you apply the guidance here, the more confident and helpful you'll become.

If you and the other parent are trying to improve the way you interact with your kids, I recommend that you refer to the book, *Connect with Your Kid*, as a guide to learn about the skills you're working on.

As you meet with your coaching partner, appreciate that it will take time for you to make new skills your habitual response. You'll need to persist as you continue to apply the skills at home and learn from your successes and frustrations. You can help each other stay positive and focused.

Also, because it's challenging to replace an old habit with a more effective one, you'll need to *work on one skill at a time*. You can help each other to stay focused. As you support each other, after several weeks you may become more comfortable with a new way of connecting with your kids. At that point, you may decide to work on another skill.

This book explains in six chapters how you can help the parent you're coaching stay on track:

1. *ACCOUNTABILITY: How This Inspires Motivation*

2. *Your Coaching Superpower:* **LISTENING**

3. *Giving Advice...**WHAT TO DO INSTEAD***

4. *LEARNING FROM EXPERIENCE...The Foundation of Skill-Building*

5. *FEEDBACK That Feels Good*

6. *ENCOURAGEMENT That Energizes*

As you read, think about how you can use these six ways to be an effective coach.

ACCOUNTABILITY: How This Inspires Motivation

Replacing an existing habit with a new skill isn't easy, because it involves going against the grain of your established habit. A current habit is a pattern of behavior that is driven by circuits in your brain, which were created by countless repetitions of the behavior over the years. To replace it with a new skill, you need to rewire your brain. This means lots of repetitions of the new behavior over time.

This can be challenging, because before a new skill is established, the old habit can automatically kick in. Or if you make mistakes and get discouraged, the danger is that you'll give up before you ingrain the new skill. A coach can help you stay positive and on track.

Holding a person accountable is powerful, because knowing someone is checking on you gives you another reason to do the hard things while making a change. You know that *they* know what you said you would do, and you know they'll ask you about it.

Knowing that someone will be checking your progress can motivate you to do the work.

It's like losing weight. If you don't stand on the scale each week to check results, it could be easy to let things slide. With the scale, you can tell whether you're actually moving forward. This form of accountability is a key element of the best weight loss programs. It inspires and motivates people to do what they said they would do until they see the results.

Here's how to set up accountability:

1. When you and another parent decide to coach each other, agree on how and when you'll make contact. Face-to-face? Phone? Email? Online? Twice a week? Monthly?

2. In your initial meeting, settle on which aspect of skill-building you want to work on. You'll need to focus—work on improving one skill at a time, so choose the skill you want to work on for the next several weeks.

3. Then the two of you agree on what you'll do to work on the skill before the next meeting. Ask each other what specific actions you'll commit to before the next meeting—exactly what, when, where, with whom, how much, and so on.

4. Keep a record of these commitments.

5. And then, the next time you meet, ask each other what you actually did and how each of these actions worked.

6. Before you conclude your coaching session, help each other reset your goals with another series of actions to accomplish before the next meeting.

Bea and Kayla meet
to hold each other
accountable....

Bea is a single mom. Her daughter is in the same fourth-grade class as Kayla's daughter. Kayla also has a twelve-year-old son. Here's how their first meeting went...

Bea: "So we're going to coach each other!"

Kayla: "Cool. Have you ever done this before?"

Bea: "No, but I've read this book, *Parents Coaching Parents*. Have you?

Kayla: "I'm into it. We're supposed to hold each other accountable."

Bea: "Right. And some other stuff. Encouraging each other."

Kayla: "I need to connect with my son better, for sure."

Bea: "I think we need to focus on one skill. What do you want to focus on?"

Kayla: "*The Connect with Your Kid* book recommends starting with listening. So I'm going with that. How about you?"

Bea: "I'm focused on listening, too. This is going to be easy."

Kayla: "I hope so."

Bea: "I've bookmarked the listening chapter. Have you read it yet?"

Kayla: "I have."

Bea: "My take is that listening is actually several skills rolled into one. What do you want to focus on?"

Kayla: "I like the bit on empathy. I've never thought of expressing empathy as a skill before, something you could get good at. So maybe I'll start with that."

Bea: "Great. I need to work on not giving advice. Just trying to hear what Olivia is trying to tell me. If I could just do that...."

Kayla: "So what are you going to try? We're supposed to actually follow the advice of the book when talking to our children. Then we get together again and talk about how it went."

Bea: "Well, I'm going to talk to Olivia after school and see what happens."

Kayla: "Cool. I'll do the same thing. I'll try to get Benjamin talking after swim practice."

Bea: "OK. So when do we talk again?"

Kayla: "How about Thursday?"

Bea: "That's fine. Text me Thursday evening when you're available."

Kayla: "OK. Maybe we'll talk every Thursday evening."

Bea: "Maybe. And hold each other accountable!"

Kayla: "Yeah! Do what we said we would do and then talk about it."

Bea: "Exactly. OK, I'll talk to you then."

Kayla: "Bye."

IN SUMMARY...

This was Bea and Kayla's first meeting, so it was brief. They set some very specific action goals, so they could start putting what they learned into practice with their kids and then talk about it at their next meeting.

Kayla called Bea on Thursday after dinner and they talked about what happened. Kayla tried the empathy techniques with Benjamin and got a mixture of reactions. Bea said she had trouble remembering to check her understanding.

They talked about why their kids reacted the way they did and what they could learn from each instance. Both decided they need more practice. Kayla remarked that the coaching felt natural to her, that talking with Bea might actually help her improve. A few months later, they were still working on aspects of listening and meeting regularly for coaching.

A Coach's Superpower: LISTENING

In your coaching role, you'll often be involved in conversation.

But you should expect that most of the time, you'll need to be *listening* instead, which is a different skill.

Most people don't think about how they listen, so they don't make a special effort to listen well. They believe it's just something you naturally do in conversation. When people talk, you listen. When you talk, they listen.

The point of listening well is to avoid misunderstanding what the other person is trying to express.

This can be easier said than done. The spoken word is never as easy to make sense of as the written word. When writing, people get to revise their message until they're sure it says what they want it to say. When coaching and being coached, you won't get to do that. Like most people, you may start with some small talk before launching into accounts of your experiences. Along the way, you might express opinions, ideas, and feelings.

All this could be revealing. But the person you're coaching may think differently than you do. There may be differences in education, skills, experience, needs, goals, values, personality—and more. They may communicate in a way that's not familiar to you. In their efforts to express themselves, they might jump back and forth in time, making it hard for you to understand the sequence. They might get to the point right away, or they might digress.

The bottom line is that the person speaking to you may not make it easy for you to understand the points they're trying to make. If you're not focused on listening well, you could misunderstand what you hear. What you think they said may not be what they meant. And there may be important things you don't hear because they're reluctant to tell you about them.

With all this going on, you'll need to be the best listener you can be, just to understand what the other person is trying to say.

The Keys to Turning On Your Listening Superpower

Here's how you can make sure you actually "get the message."

1. ***Recognize when it's time to listen***

   Be aware when the person you're coaching is about to tell you something about their learning. In other words, be alert to when it's time to *stop conversing* and *start listening*.

2. ***Focus your attention***

   When listening, don't do anything else. Don't multitask or let anything distract you—not even your thoughts. Let the other person do most of the talking. Listening is mostly about being quiet and focusing on them. It's not about telling your own stories, giving your own opinions, laying out your reasoning, offering your ideas, or giving advice. Your brain needs to be focused on making sense of what the other person is trying to express. Even if your knowledge, experience and wisdom kick in and you feel a powerful impulse to give your two cents, don't do it. And be careful not to interrupt. Interrupting is a tell-tale sign that you aren't listening. So while they're talking, make the speaker feel like they're the most important person in your world.

3. Listen for the meaning

Think about what the person is saying and how they're saying it in order to understand *why* they're saying it—the point they're trying to make. Make an effort to pick up on both verbal and nonverbal messages. Consider their tone of voice, facial expressions, gestures, and other body language. If they're sharing their feelings, do your best to express empathy.

4. Check the meaning

When you think you understand some of what the speaker has said, don't assume you got it right. Check the message. To be sure, tell the speaker—in your own words—what you think you've understood so far:

- "You seem to be saying that...."
- "Do you mean...."
- "It sounds like...."
- "So you...."
- "You feel that...."
- "Do I understand that...."

5. *Ask for more information*

The person you're coaching will let you know whether you got it right. Either way, encourage them to continue, so you can listen for more meaning and check again. Continue checking until you're sure you've understood the whole message.

As you can see from this way of listening, there's more to it than just paying attention. It's an active process in which you try to grasp the point they're trying to make, while checking to be sure you've understood it correctly. If you listen this way, you'll know whether you "got the message." And the speaker will know it, too—which will be gratifying for both of you.

People love being
heard.

Mariko listens to her husband Joe....

Mariko and Joe have been married for sixteen years. Mariko persuaded Joe to read *Connect with Your Kid* and work with her as they both try to nurture their relationship with Buddy, their twelve-year old son, who is now in middle school. During their latest weekly accountability meeting, she listened to Joe talk about his efforts to encourage Buddy...

Joe: "Yesterday, I had a golden opportunity to give Buddy feedback."

Mariko: "Great! How did it go?"

Joe: "You and I talked about how he neglects his chores."

Mariko: "Yeah. Especially gathering the trash and putting it out for pickup."

Joe: "Right. I reminded him about it, and he got all defensive."

Mariko: "So he didn't like your feedback. What did he say?"

Joe: "He said he takes care of it most of the time. And he says he's been really busy with schoolwork and basketball practice. He complained that I'm too rigid about it and I should give him some slack. And so on."

Mariko: "Why do you think Buddy reacted that way?"

Joe: "I think he sees my feedback as undeserved criticism."

Mariko: "So he thinks you're too hard on him. What do you think?"

Joe: "Well, he needs us to hold him accountable. It must be my approach. Maybe I'm doing something wrong."

Mariko: "You think you need to read that chapter on feedback again?"

Joe: "Maybe. Something about sandwiching my feedback between two positives that I'm not getting right."

Mariko: "Affirming the good and giving encouragement at the end."

Joe: "Yeah, like that. I need to do that better."

Mariko: "So you plan to review."

Joe: "Yeah. How about you? Have you cut back on giving advice?"

Mariko: "The book says to ask open-ended questions instead, to get them to think. I know how to do that, and it's a great idea. But I forget. Giving advice is what I've always thought a smart mom was supposed to do. Like it's how I pass on what I have to offer. It's kind of a habit."

Joe: "You want to remember to ask questions instead. But you catch yourself giving advice too late."

Mariko: "It's frustrating. It's embarrassing."

Joe: "You feel like giving up."

Mariko: "No, actually I feel like trying harder. For heaven's sake, it's not rocket science. I can do this."

Joe: "So you plan to double down on your goal for the coming week."

Mariko: "I do."

Joe: "I'm eager to hear how it goes. We both have to double down, I think."

Mariko: "We do. Let's talk again next week. Let's talk about our successes for a change."

Joe: "I'm in."

IN SUMMARY...

In their weekly accountability huddle, both Joe and Mariko admitted to coming up short applying what they learned about communicating with their son, Buddy. Both of them did a good job of listening to their spouse's frustrations. Joe resolved to review the description of feedback in the book, *Connect with Your Kid*. And Mariko resolved to keep trying to catch herself before giving advice and instead to encourage Buddy to think for himself.

Giving Advice...
WHAT TO DO
INSTEAD

There are problems with giving advice. For one thing, your suggestion may not be the best one for the person you're coaching. You weren't there to experience their situation, so you don't have all the facts. If they follow your advice and it doesn't work for them, you bear some responsibility for that. Also, giving advice doesn't give them credit for their ability to work through their own issues. If they make mistakes, learning from them is a valuable part of skill-building. And when they're successful, you don't want them to give you the credit; you want them to feel a sense of ownership and self-confidence.

So, if you feel the urge to offer a suggestion or an idea, what's a more helpful approach?

The answer: *ask open-ended questions to get them to think.*

In other words, stay away from questions that can be an-

When coaching, you may get an idea or think of a helpful solution.

Resist the urge to give advice. Instead, encourage the other person to do their own thinking.

swered with a fact or a simple "yes" or "no." Questions that probe for facts can bring communication to a halt. For example, if they answer, "Yesterday about two-thirty," you have to get the interaction going again.

When the person you're coaching has finished making a point and you have confirmed that you understand, ask questions that encourage them to continue explaining. Also, you may sense that they're faced with certain issues or challenges. Don't take ownership by offering your own ideas. Instead, encourage the speaker to think about possible solutions. Some examples:

- "Then what happened?"

- "How do you feel about that?"

- "Can you give me an example?"

- "What's your opinion?"

- "What have you tried?"

Nearly always, a person can reason through to solutions, so the best thing you can do is to encourage them to do their own thinking. But on occasion, someone could be genuinely stumped. They may be at a total loss to know what to do, and they may beg for your advice. In this case, you'll have to make a judgment call. While it may be helpful to share your experience, you need to be cautious. Qualify what you say with something like this: *"I'm not sure what your situation is like, but this has worked for me...."*

Chris and Rodrigo coach each other to think....

Two old friends, encouraged by their wives, are coaching each other to work on family communication. Chris is the father of a ten-year-old girl. Rodrigo is the father of a three-year-old girl and a thirteen-year-old boy. During their regular golf outings, they check on each other's progress...

Chris: "Whassup, my man?"

Rodrigo: "Success."

Chris: "Whoa! Progress! Tell me about it."

Rodrigo: "You know I planned to practice listening with my boy, Arturo. The problem is, he's kind of an introvert. Always on his phone and doesn't talk much. So I decided to practice with my wife Jackie instead. We talk all the time. I figure it doesn't matter who I practice with. If I get better talking with Jackie, I can use the skills with Arturo."

Chris: "And...."

Rodrigo: "It worked."

Chris: "Tell me about it."

Rodrigo: "Well, I've been trying to get better at expressing empathy, something I've never tried to do. It's a stretch!"

Chris: "And...."

Rodrigo: "And I pulled it off, man. She was complaining about the long lines at the grocery store. What I felt like telling her was, 'Hey Honey, you just gotta be patient.' But I didn't. Instead, I said, 'I know, it's got to be frustrating to just stand there waiting when you have so much to do.'"

Chris: "How did she respond to that?"

Rodrigo: "It was amazing. She just smiled and said, 'That's right,' and quit complaining. I tried it again later. She was clearing the table after dinner and said, 'One more mess for me to clean up.' So I kind of put myself in her shoes and said, 'It feels unfair to do most of the cooking and then be left to clean up. I bet it would be nice to have a little help.' And she just came over and hugged me."

Chris: "Wow, you're getting good at this."

Rodrigo: "Now I'm wondering what would happen if I tried some empathy with Arturo."

Chris: "Is that your plan for the coming week?"

Rodrigo: "Why not? Sure. So how about you? You resolved any conflicts lately?"

Chris: "Not exactly. What the book says about conflict resolution makes sense, but I'm not sure how to get my girl to think about her needs instead of her wants. And I haven't given much thought to what *I* need. You know, instead of what I want *her* to do. I think I'm going to need a lot more practice."

Rodrigo: "So no success stories this week. You plan to stay with this skill?"

Chris: "I really want to master this. Tanya and I don't always see eye to eye. If we can learn how to give a little, I feel it would be a good thing. And I want to get good at this in my selling."

Rodrigo: "Sure. Why not? So that's your plan?"

Chris: "Yeah."

Rodrigo: "OK. Let's talk again in a couple weeks. And let's have some success stories to talk about."

Chris: "You got it."

IN SUMMARY...

Chris and Rodrigo have been golfing buddies for years. So they decided they would have accountability discussions while on the golf course. In this conversation, both of them refrained from giving advice. Instead, they encouraged each other to think about what to do next.

LEARNING FROM EXPERIENCE...
The Foundation of Skill-Building

People don't always learn from what happens to them. You have many experiences every day. But to capture the lessons, you have to consciously think about what happened and why. If you don't, it's possible that you won't learn much from your experience, and you might repeat your mistakes.

Experience really is the best teacher. People can learn important lessons from what happens to them. But sometimes they don't.

Consciously learning from experience not only helps you get better at what you're doing, it can accelerate your skill development. You and your coaching partner can help each other reflect by asking open-ended questions like these:

1. **What happened?** The details need to be recalled in order to make sense of them. What was the sequence of events? What did you do? How did others react? How do you feel about it?

2. **Why did you handle it this way?** Things happen for a reason. To imagine a better way to handle a situation like this, try to understand why things occurred the way they did. What helped or hindered? What led to the outcome?

3. **What were the consequences?** Appreciating the impact of what happened creates the motivation to handle situations like this more effectively. Benefits? Costs? Problems? Resolutions?

4. **How would you handle a similar situation in the future?** What did you learn from this experience? What basic principles? How are you going to apply the lesson?

5. **What are your next steps?** What will you do going forward to implement this learning?

These questions have a logical sequence; but when coaching, the other person might begin connecting the dots without your help. They might even skip a step and jump to what they learned.

People aren't perfect, and it's hard to change a habit. Mistakes and failures can be steps toward growth. If you learn from what happens and if you persist, the percentage of successes will increase. The key is to learn something from every success and every shortfall.

Liz and Jack help
each other discover
the lesson....

After Liz read through *Connect with Your Kid*, she asked her husband, Jack, to do the same, saying she'd like them to coach each other. Jack agreed. Later, during a conversation between them, Jack described a confrontation with their daughter, Carly...

Jack: "Did you know Carly wants to go to Germany with her German class?"

Liz: "She mentioned it to me."

Jack: "What did you tell her?"

Liz: "I just said I'd talk to you about it."

Jack: "Well, besides not being able to afford it, I don't think she's ready to go on a trip like that."

Liz: "So what did you tell her?"

Jack: "It took me by surprise. I didn't know what to say or how to respond. I kind of had a mind-freeze. I just smiled and said I'd think about it. I know I'm supposed to be working on dialogue right now, but I wasn't sure what skill was best in that situation. Does it call for dialogue, or conflict resolution, or getting her to think?"

Liz: "Ha! That's interesting. Have you thought about it? What skill do you think was best in that situation?"

Jack: "I guess maybe it wouldn't make much difference. Maybe any of those skills would have worked. Plus listening."

Liz: "Maybe. You'll need to get back to her. Will you go with dialogue, since that's what you're focused on these days?"

Jack: "That sounds good. I can start with how I feel about it. Then ask for her opinion. And listen and see how it goes."

Liz: "Sounds like your goal for this week."

Jack: "Okay. How did you do with your listening?"

Liz: "I think I'm really getting the hang of it. I'm pretty good with empathy, so I usually lead with that. Yesterday she was complaining about having to share the cost of a new cell phone. So instead of lecturing her about responsibility, cell phone ownership, and so on, I just said, 'You're trying to save your money and the idea of giving up twenty dollars a month is distressing.' It was as if a door opened. I asked her, 'What are your thoughts about cell phone ownership?'"

Jack: "Cool."

Liz: "So then I tried to understand what she was getting at, and checked the message a couple times. Jack, you know what she said?"

Jack: "No, what?"

Liz: "She said, 'Mom, you really get me.'"

Jack: "Wow."

Liz: "I know. I thought I was going to tear up."

Jack: "So, Babe, you're a listening pro now, right?"

Liz: "Truthfully, I think I know what I'm doing now, but I don't think I own it yet. It's not me yet. I sometimes forget. I need more practice."

Jack: "Sounds like this week you plan to look for more opportunities to listen."

Liz: "That's where I am."

Jack: "Hey. An idea."

Liz: "Okay."

Jack: "Feel free to practice some of that great listening on me."

Liz: "Ha! That's a good idea! I'll do that."

Jack: "Great. Then I'll be able to give you some feedback."

Liz: "I'm counting on it."

IN SUMMARY...

Liz and Jack have enthusiastically bought into the idea of coaching each other as they try to improve their communication skills. Jack faltered when his daughter hit him with her desire to take an overseas trip with her class. His first reaction was the thought that she wasn't ready to handle herself in that situation. It caught him off guard, he wasn't sure how to react, and he lost the opportunity to initiate dialogue. Liz helped him think through what to do next.

Liz, on the other hand, had a success story. Jack asked her about moving on to another skill, but she concluded that she needed more successes to feel confident.

You can tell from these examples that sometimes coaching is just helping people pick themselves up from frustrations and getting back on track. One of the most helpful things you can do in situations like this is to offer feedback that encourages. How to do this effectively is the topic of the next chapter.

FEEDBACK
THAT FEELS GOOD

5

Feedback isn't criticism. The best feedback
addresses behavior in a way that builds a
person up.

Not every coach has the advantage of observing the person they're coaching. If you don't have first-hand knowledge of how the other person goes about being a parent, it wouldn't be appropriate for you to give them feedback. Leave that to the people who do observe them. On the other hand, you *can* give effective feedback if you're able to observe someone's behavior in action. In that case, this chapter will be helpful. So read on!

There's a big difference between criticism and feedback. Criticism is an expression of displeasure. Criticism happens when you're so put off with what a person has done that you let your anger take over and verbally attack them. I'm talking about things like put-downs, name-calling, and sarcasm. The assault could be disguised as a toxic question, such as "What's the matter with you?" or "Why did you do that?" Criticism is negative and mean-spirited.

But letting a person know when their behavior is causing problems can be helpful. The key is to hold a mirror up to their behavior in a way that builds them up, rather than tears them down.

There are three easy ways to do this. The first is known as "constructive feedback." The method is quite easy: *sandwich your feedback between two positives.*

Step 1: Affirm the good. You don't want to sugar-coat your feedback, but if you only mention the unwanted behavior, it will make the person think you haven't noticed the good things they've done. They'll sense you're being unfair and want to discount your feedback. To defuse defensiveness, before you give your feedback, mention at least one thing related to the actions at hand that you appreciate. For example: "Hal, most of the time you're very supportive of what your child is doing."

Step 2: Describe specifically the problem behavior. To do this, you need to have observed the event first-hand. You can't rely on what others have said; if they've observed it, it's their job to give the feedback. *And the description needs to be specific.* For example, "Jess needed your help yesterday and you didn't make time for her."

Step 3: Explain the impact. Describe the consequences of the behavior. For example: "She ended up making the same mistake all over again."

Step 4: Reset expectations. Discuss with the other person what they could have done instead. For example: "You've often gone the extra mile for me when I needed help. How could you have handled this differently?"

Step 5: Encourage and offer support. These positives are the other piece of the sandwich. For example: "I see you as the kind of dad who wants to have your kid's back when they need it."

Another kind of feel-good feedback is affirming something done well: praise, recognition, acknowledgment—any kind of feedback that focuses on someone's effort or achievement. Like constructive feedback, positive feedback describes specific behavior. A general comment such as "Great job!" might feel good, but if you want to encourage more of that kind of behavior in the future, it helps if the person knows exactly what was appreciated. For example: "Candy, I loved the way you handled that situation. You got right to the point and gave some good examples of what you wanted."

A third kind of feedback is called "feedforward," because it doesn't focus on past behavior. Instead, it focuses on the future, mentioning specific actions that you'd like to see more of. For example: "Terry, just now you described that situation in a lot of detail, which helped me understand where you're coming from. I'd appreciate more of that in our discussions."

As I mentioned upfront in this chapter, your relationship with the parent you're coaching may be such that you rarely see them in action. But if you ever have the occasion to observe behavior and give feedback, here are a few tips to make sure it builds them up:

- Keep the feedback private
- Check that the person is ready to hear it
- Make it as fresh and timely as possible
- Focus on one issue at a time
- Be honest
- Own your feedback
- If the person responds, listen to understand

Clay holds a mirror up to J.T.'s behavior —in a nice way....

Clay and J.T. are an example of two dads who agreed to coach each other while working on the skills in *Connect with Your Kid*. They recently met after work for a beer in Clay's back yard...

Clay: "J.T."

J.T.: "Clay."

Clay: "I'm going to hold you accountable today, man."

J.T.: "Counting on it, dude."

Clay: "Good. Hey, tell me what happened with you and Shawna. You said she's been thinking about quitting the tennis team."

J.T.: "I told you she's been down because she hasn't won a single set in practice. Now she thinks the coach is going to cut her, and so she might as well give it up and move on."

Clay: "So how did you handle it?"

J.T.: "I think giving up at this point would be bad for her. It's a chance for her to work harder and turn it into her own success story. It would be good for her self-confidence. I told her, 'If you quit now, you'll see yourself as a loser.'"

Clay: "I'll bet she didn't like that."

J.T.: "Yeah, she started crying, and I told her crying is for losers."

Clay: "How did that work out?"

J.T.: "We're not talking anymore. She has to figure this out for herself."

Clay: "J.T.?"

J.T.: "Yeah?"

Clay: "I want to give you some feedback."

J.T.: "Really? OK, shoot."

Clay: "This was the week you were going to encourage Shawna. I know your heart's in the right place and you've made a commitment to work on how you encourage your daughter. But hey, man, what you said doesn't sound like encouragement to me. Not even close."

J.T.: "Look, Trish and I've been putting up with her whining. I just decided she needs somebody to call her out. Get tough with her."

Clay: "I hear you. You feel that letting her whine hasn't helped. But how long has it been since you read that chapter on encouragement?"

J.T.: "I don't remember. Are you saying I should go back and review it?"

Clay: "I don't remember anything in it that sounds like tough love."

J.T.: "OK. My input isn't working. Maybe the book has some tips."

Clay: "So what's your plan?"

J.T.: "I'll check that chapter again. I need something that will work. What we're doing isn't working."

Clay: "Sounds good. I know you and Trish want Shawna to succeed."

J.T.: "We do. Thanks, bro."

Clay: "By the way, this was my week for practicing feedback. Did you notice I just gave you some feedback? How did it feel?"

J.T.: "Hey, you're right! That was some feedback, all right. Yeah, it felt OK. It felt positive. You kind of got in my face, but you didn't criticize me. You did good!"

Clay: "Thanks. Ha! You just gave me feedback about my feedback!"

J.T.: "Just holding each other accountable, coach."

Clay: "Thanks. But I need more practice. I'm going to look for more chances to give feedback. Maybe at work."

J.T.: "And I definitely need to try something different to encourage Shawna. I guess we have our marching orders."

Clay: "I guess we do."

IN SUMMARY...

Clay and J.T. both served in Iraq and have been friends for years, so they're able to be honest with each other without worrying about being offended. J.T. had been frustrated with his daughter's negative attitude, and he decided to confront her the same way his squad members used to deal with each other in combat. Clay felt this approach wouldn't help the young girl, so using what he learned about feedback, he urged his friend to go back to the text and review tips for giving encouragement. Then he asked for feedback about his feedback. In all, a useful accountability session!

For more feedback tips, read Chapter 10 of *Connect with Your Kid*. You'll learn more about encouragement—the other half of the "feedback sandwich"—in the next section.

ENCOURAGEMENT
That Energizes

Even a strong, capable parent can get discouraged. You may be resilient, but sometimes unexpected mistakes or difficulties can take the wind out of your sails and make you doubt yourself. A series of stumbles can cause you to be so disheartened that you want to give up. You can lose sight of what's possible, feeling that continuing to strive isn't worth the effort. You "lose heart."

This is what we call *discouragement*.

If this happens to the person you're coaching, you can help them recover.

Most people have the idea that offering encouragement is a no-brainer, that if you care about someone, encouragement comes naturally. However, there's a best way to help a dispirited person.

First, appreciate that there are mistaken ways to encourage

It's easy to give the kind of encouragement that actually lifts a person up.

that can have the opposite effect. The classic mistake is false assurance. Has anyone ever told you that "everything is going to be all right"? Even though they may have offered it with a kind spirit, statements like this are empty if they have no basis.

Another way some people try to encourage is to sugarcoat reality. Someone might say, "This isn't so bad." Downplaying an unpleasant truth is common enough, but anyone who's been brought to their knees by adversity knows that denying it doesn't help.

Some people think encouragement means taking a tough-love approach, when they say something like, "Come on, stuff happens. Get over it."

Discouragement happens when an adverse situation causes someone to be so focused on their frustration and the negatives that they're no longer acknowledging the positives of their situation—even though the upsides are real and valid. Every situation is a mixture of negative and positive elements: challenges and opportunities; problems and solutions; advantages and disadvantages; mistakes and lessons learned.

As with any communication skill, the first step is to notice when the parent you're coaching is feeling down. Your job will be to help them recover a balanced perspective—one that reminds them that there's both good and bad in their situation. You can use any of these elements of encouragement in any order:

- Listen with empathy to understand
- Affirm their strengths
- Point out the positives to restore a balanced perspective
- Offer support

What You Can Do When Someone Loses Heart

1. Listen with empathy to understand

Listening is first on this list because when you listen, you find out how discouraged the person is and what happened to cause it. Listening isn't about telling the person what they should be thinking, feeling or doing. Instead, you focus your attention, sense their feelings, listen for the meaning, and check what you hear.

It's okay if the individual starts "venting." This is a good sign. They may need to get their feelings of frustration off their chest, and they may feel relieved afterward. It may be all they need to "snap out of it."

2. Affirm their strengths

Nobody's perfect. Everyone is a unique blend of strengths and weaknesses. The idea is to affirm their strengths. When things go wrong, the person you're coaching might blame themselves. They may experience a blow to their self-esteem and self-confidence. They may temporarily lose sight of who they are and what they're capable of.

Your job is to remind them of their strengths. They will probably be focused on the failure at hand, not their past achievements;

so it can help to bring up examples of where they've succeeded before in equally tough or even tougher situations.

3. Point out the positives to restore a balanced perspective

In addition to a negative view of themselves, a discouraged individual may also focus on the negatives in their situation—what caused their distress. To restore a balanced, realistic perspective, acknowledge the negatives; and then remind them that the situation isn't all negative. There are also advantages, potentials, opportunities, resources and other upsides. The positives are real, too.

4. Offer support

When someone has been discouraged by difficulty or failure, they may wonder if you still believe in their ability to succeed. If you sense this self-doubt, reassure them that you're still very much in their corner.

Luna gives Sheryl some encouragement....

On their accountability day, Luna sensed that Sheryl was dispirited...

Luna: "You seem down today."

Sheryl: "Mmm."

Luna: "What's up?"

Sheryl: "I've been trying to get Jordan fired up. It's as if he doesn't care about school anymore. He's so bright and capable of doing so much. I don't think of him as being lazy. It's just that I'd like him to get motivated again."

Luna: "Okay."

Sheryl: "But nothing's working."

Luna: "Can you give me an example?"

Sheryl: "Sure. He has a paper due in two weeks, and he's procrastinating. I know what will happen. He'll wait until the last minute and stay up most of the night. No way he'll get a good grade doing that. I've been trying to get him to start now. But he just makes excuses."

Luna: "So you're stuck."

Sheryl: "Right. I feel like giving up on him."

Luna: "It must be discouraging to try so hard to help him and have him not respond."

Sheryl: "I don't know what to do."

Luna: "No wonder you're bummed out. Sorry, gal."

Sheryl: "But where does that leave me?"

Luna: "Well, for starters, I bet you've found ways to fire up others at work."

Sheryl: "Sure, but this is my son. He's a kid, a work in process. This is different."

Luna: "Sheryl, I see you as a creative, persistent kind of person. I don't see you giving up on Jordan."

Sheryl: "I don't think I'm giving up. I love Jordan. I'm just not sure what will work with him."

Luna: "These past several weeks you've tried to get Jordan to buy into the importance of his schoolwork. It sounds like he hasn't been buying in."

Sheryl: "That's a good way of putting it."

Luna: "Maybe you haven't been thinking about Jordan in terms of buy-in. What can you do differently to get him to buy in?"

Sheryl: "Good question. I need some ideas."

Luna: "Have you considered going back to the book?"

Sheryl: "You know, I probably should do that. I haven't looked at it for several weeks."

Luna: "Are we still on for next Friday? Is this your goal for the week, to mine the book for more ideas to inspire Jordan to buy in? And then see if they work?"

Sheryl: "That's a good plan."

Luna: "You're one of the smartest people I know. I'm sure you'll come up with something that'll work."

Sheryl: "Thanks, Luna. I'm going to give it a try."

IN SUMMARY...

Sheryl was discouraged, but she's a self-starter and it didn't take much to re-energize her. All Luna had to do was a bit of listening, while affirming her and her situation. Luna remembered to clarify Sheryl's goal for the week, which they would talk about at the next meeting.

Keep in mind that replacing an old habit with an effective skill can be a challenging journey. Some people handle mistakes, failures, and frustrations better than others. If you sense that the person you're coaching is feeling discouraged, you can help them get back up, dust themselves off, and keep trying. You can learn more about encouragement in Chapter 8 of *Connect with Your Kid*.

You Can Do It!

So, can you do this—play the role of parent coach?
Of course you can!

This book focuses on six helpful things you can do when coaching another parent:

- Coach them to set specific action goals and hold them accountable

- Listen to "get the message" when the person you're coaching is trying to tell you something

- Get them to do their own thinking

- Help them learn from their experiences interacting with their child

- If you've observed their efforts, give helpful feedback

- Offer encouragement when needed

Now that you've read *Parents Coaching Parents*, keep it handy and refer to it as you prepare for your coaching meetings. Think about how you can apply the six helpful actions in the sequence of a typical peer coaching session:

- Hold them accountable. Ask if they did what they committed to do during the last session. How did it go?

- Listen with empathy to understand.

- Ask questions that help them learn from their experience.

- Offer encouragement.

- Guide them to commit to their next set of actions, and take notes so you can hold them accountable at the next meeting.

One of the wonderful benefits of parents coaching parents is that while you're getting better at it, you'll be helping the other parent get better at helping you.

Connect with
Your Kid

In this book, to illustrate how parents can effectively coach each other, I've frequently referred to the book, ***Connect with Your Kid: Mastering the Top 10 Parent-Child Communication Skills***.

Its purpose is to be a guide for parents who want to grow the bond with their children by improving the way they interact with them.

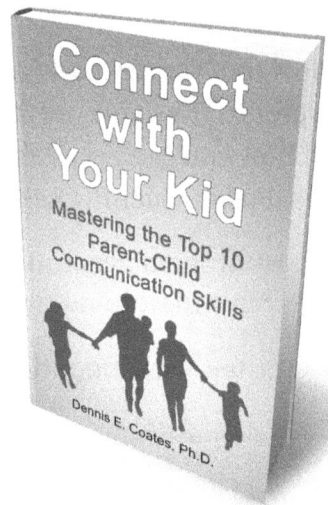

When we were growing up, no one taught us the best ways to listen, give feedback, offer encouragement, and other key aspects of interpersonal communication. And yet, parents impact their kids through countless interactions every day.

This is why parents need to improve the way they relate to their children. ***Connect with Your Kid*** is a unique how-to handbook for what I've learned through the decades are the skills that matter most.

It's possible for parents to successfully improve the way they connect with their kids by practicing the skills described in the book. Doing this involves replacing existing relationship habits with new, improved ones. With a concentrated effort, any parent can succeed; but it will take commitment, time, and persistence.

It's so much easier to make this effort if you don't have do it alone. Your chances of success are vastly improved if you have someone to hold you accountable and encourage you. While **Connect with Your Kid** is an ideal guide for working on being a more effective parent, self-development is a journey; and I wrote **Parents Coaching Parents** so you can get the support you need.

By the way, I've coauthored similar books for the workplace, **Connect with Your Team** (with Meredith Bell), and **Peer Coaching Made Simple**.

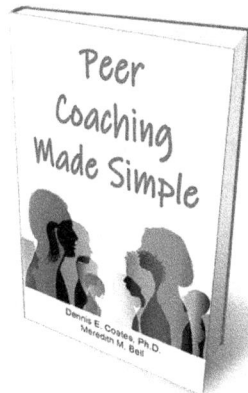

Dennis E. Coates, Ph.D.
Meredith M. Bell

Connect
with
Your Team

Mastering the Top 10
Communication Skills

Peer
Coaching
Made Simple

Dennis E. Coates, Ph.D.
Meredith M. Bell

Dennis E. Coates, Ph.D.

Dr. Denny Coates is an expert in parent-child communication and adolescent brain development. He is the author of several books and hundreds of articles for parents. His two latest books, *Connect with Your Kid: Mastering the Top 10 Parent-Child Communication Skills* and *Parents Coaching Parents*, provide a practical, step-by-step approach that helps parents build a bond with their child that lasts a lifetime. You can find information about his books and other resources at DrDennyCoates.com.

He is the father of two grown sons, and he lives with his wife, Kathleen Scott, near San Antonio, Texas.

Website & blog: https://DrDennyCoates.com
LinkedIn: DrDennyCoates
Twitter: @DrDennyCoates

Denny is available as a podcast guest and as a speaker at corporate or association events.

Quantity sales. Special discounts are available on quantity purchases by corporations, associations and others. For details, contact us at info@growstrongleaders.com or 757-656-4765.

www.ingramcontent.com/pod-product-compliance
Lightning Source LLC
Chambersburg PA
CBHW071733020426
42331CB00008B/2012